WORDS OF THE CHAMPIONS
YOUR KEY TO THE BEE

2021

Contents

Developed by the Scripps National Spelling Bee

Greetings, Champions!

About this Study Guide

Do you dream of winning a school spelling bee, or even attending the Scripps National Spelling Bee? *Words of the Champions* is the official study resource of the Scripps National Spelling Bee, so you've found the perfect place to start. Prepare for a 2021 or 2021 classroom, grade-level, school, district, county, regional or state spelling bee with this list of 4,000 words.

All words in this book have been selected by the Scripps National Spelling Bee from our official dictionary, *Merriam-Webster Unabridged* (http://unabridged.merriam-webster.com).

Words of the Champions is divided into three difficulty levels, ranked One Bee (800 words), Two Bee (2,100 words) and Three Bee (1,200 words). These are great words to challenge you, whether you're just getting started in spelling bees or of if you've already participated in several. At the beginning of each level, you'll find the *School Spelling Bee Study List* words. For any classroom, grade-level or school spelling bee, study the 125-word One Bee *School Spelling Bee Study List*, the 225-word Two Bee *School Spelling Bee Study List* and the 100-word Three Bee *School Spelling Bee Study List:* a total of 450 words.

Following the *School Spelling Bee Study List* in each level, you'll find pages marked "Words of the Champions." Are you a school spelling bee champion or a speller advancing to compete beyond the school level? Study these pages to make sure you're prepared to do your best when these words are asked in the early rounds of competition. And remember, although spelling bees will start with words from this guide, they often end with words you haven't studied.

Each year, the Scripps National Spelling Bee will release a new version of *Words of the Champions* featuring 800 new words, including an all-new *School Spelling Bee Study List*.

Your spelling bee journey starts now, and taking the first step toward becoming a star athlete of the English language makes you a *Champion*. These *Words* are for you.

About the Scripps National Spelling Bee

The Scripps National Spelling Bee is the nation's largest and longest-running educational program. The purpose of the Scripps National Spelling Bee is to help students improve their spelling, increase their vocabularies, learn concepts and develop correct English usage that will help them all their lives.

Visit spellingbee.com for more information about the Bee and to check if your school is enrolled. The Scripps National Spelling Bee is administered on a not-for-profit basis by The E.W. Scripps Company.

Difficulty Level: One Bee
School Spelling Bee Study List

gel	mugs	chess
train	fair	slimy
sport	dinner	squeak
rich	rats	friend
eel	fed	laptop
fans	sir	movie
dome	boom	known
tall	wave	suffer
better	trunk	double
hit	sleepy	watch
peanut	full	ahoy
cake	huge	dream
bite	born	whine
noon	jumping	beans
gummy	damp	child
sting	from	space
ray	hunch	princess
dusk	each	piper
mops	shade	hear
thanks	ribs	sprint
dash	forever	awe
skin	freeze	afar
star	scorch	bowl
began	motor	sweat
grew	talking	cost
fine	money	sleek
day	couch	bottle
upset	nibble	smart
father	strands	stared
jam	chapter	plopped

darted	December	swirled
angry	sudden	amount
sidekick	slither	sighed
stuff	combed	sheen
least	patrol	worse
little	epic	sandwich
felt	vital	duo
summer	window	gleaming
carefully	pocket	repress
would	project	clothes
shambles	goofy	either
taillight	remember	rely
quicken	travel	chose
presence	cranky	belle
sizzle	career	else
hatchling	disease	picture
razz	trophy	prepare
followed	theater	percent
purple	OR theatre	afraid
entire	athlete	rescue
	jotted	

Great Words, Great Works Reading Program

Each year, the Scripps National Spelling Bee publishes its School Spelling Bee Study List to help students prepare for classroom and school-level spelling bees. These words come from a list of books carefully selected by the Bee's editorial team. That list of books is called Great Words, Great Works. Find it at spellingbee.com/book-list.

Difficulty Level: One Bee
Words of the Champions

gradual	turtle	bogus
ferocious	Pinkerton	recoup
frequently	fortune	bookworm
permission	sluggard	veteran
towel	bedlam	erase
sundae	shortfall	handcuffs
ornament	cowlick	spinal
rooster	opinionated	demolition
scold	slogan	gargantuan
organza	triumphant	salsa
fragile	parenthetic	chaotic
galaxy	listener	shrimp
complaint	guardian	mandate
curries	dwindled	turret
tennis	fraught	pigeon
grumbling	sturdy	satellite
garlic	treadmill	parasite
hula	originate	favorite
reactionary	forfend	OR *favourite
muscular	OR forefend	cascade
drizzle	eavesdrop	dandelion
accurate	January	famous
studio	scruple	pristine
illusionist	moxie	golden
genetic	winnow	modesty
levity	incentive	amphibian
moisture	admirer	jealousy
toughness	emotional	remedial
tasteless	chia	vouch
astute	raspberry	trivia

*chiefly British spelling

shoulder	freight	genius
zebra	honeybee	nuance
butterscotch	blemish	stencil
apron	crumpet	penguin
beagle	blizzard	freckle
kidney	squirm	blooper
wistful	harmonious	misconception
raven	lawyer	lambkin
fructose	valiant	chowder
Amazon	purse	sunflower
companion	raisin	lambasted
panorama	trumpet	volumetric
gimmick	bias	flattery
flannel	lettuce	simmer
cucumber	shamrock	whisk
McMansion	Americana	bathtub
janitor	monopolize	fantastically
lionize	water	failure
headdress	marathon	tolerable
vault	omission	mosquito
pear	newbie	target
system	spreadsheet	angora
pedigree	badger	snippet
empty	fortification	ascribe
amulet	hydra	hodgepodge
guess	grouse	verbiage
magician	manta	nephew
carrot	astonish	imbibe
meteor	fashionista	savvy
distraught	stubble	reckon

In Good Company

When it comes to spelling bee participants, the more the merrier! In fact, more than 11 million spellers participate in qualifying spelling bees throughout the country and around the world.

---

boorish
tarmac
iteration
nurture
volcano
forensics
miraculous
trendy
permafrost
iceberg

cactus
nationalism
leeway
pilferer
rollicking
quart
lactose
domineering
onion
abandon

nervily
junior
hamlet
jubilant
thawed
uncle
dawdle
mogul
troll
kindred

tantrum
science
cement
venomous
plaintiff
mayhem
thicket
gymnastics
island
peacenik

ounce
memorandum
bother
missile
munchkin
banana
furnace
foothills
tongue
caterpillar

wasp
kudos
alpha
shebang
tibia
hazelnut
votive
lantern
mince
bubbly

graham
headlong
timber
medallion
maximum
clover
casino
distinctive
mister
warning

useful
difficult
mischief
talent
kiwi
publish
mutter
sedentary
divine
lexicon

bristle
daresay
owlishly
criminal
recipient
strong
canteen
aviation
lucky
rocket

reflect	measly	primatologist
scent	apprehensive	voluntary
puzzles	zither	furious
scumble	whiff	wombat
extinct	lamentable	marginalize
jersey	brilliant	swipe
trapezoid	competitive	eternity
dillydally	lounge	imagery
haggle	supper	pastel
sword	explosive	twice
mastiff	cajole	megahertz
cooperate	bauble	gnash
merchandise	happenstance	knuckle
gauntlet	tussle	bribery
apology	inched	glucose
carnival	dimension	mower
buffoonery	ugliness	campus
intellectual	quack	infant
tickled	spider	thunderbolt
domino	weather	despicable
ignite	twinge	elderly
legacy	poncho	amigo
splurge	hooligan	bestow
neigh	decade	gung ho
cabbage	forbidden	umbrella
erode	jumbo	synthetic
formalize	mortal	cloying
OR *formalise	bugaboo	olive
anyway	standard	truth
isolation	yearn	balderdash

*chiefly British spelling

Our Namesake

Although the first national spelling bee occurred in 1925, it wasn't until 1941 that Scripps-Howard Newspapers, now known as The E.W. Scripps Company, assumed leadership of the program.

infringe
interloper
routine
privacy
decision
farfetched
linen
piratical
pigsty
misery

months
guffaw
caravan
culinary
boycott
calzone
bawl
circle
respect
introverted

fuddy-duddy
pulley
Kodiak
misinterpret
twee
holiday
indigo
forage
tooth
dauntlessly

faucet
scheme
cough
straw
hooves
shadow
meekness
squall
OR squawl
omen
militant

civics
locker
jabberwocky
detention
sparkle
calico
theme
literacy
loathe
axle

glimmer
vacation
napkin
overrun
yellowfin
clodhopper
crayon
bakery
porridge
eyelet

yeti
groove
estimate
cattail
paraphrase
heartthrob
cheek
daughter
laser
invoke

upshot
climate
Yankee
dim sum
moose
cuckoo
dilemma
outrageous
silver
fedora

wildcat
monstrosity
sofa
eggplant
kosher
minority
default
heroic
bombard
furtive

journal	twitchy	dough
tulip	arrogant	emperor
myself	normative	utterable
marine	homework	leniency
cloudy	mildew	frivolous
cricket	pattern	potato
motto	coffee	wholehearted
torch	botch	metadata
pamper	receptacle	farewell
pleasant	bagpipe	hypnotic
robin	bonfire	jewel
historical	abruptly	tangible
rules	bushel	nourish
geometric	skedaddle	vulpine
villa	toddler	aloha
midriff	everglades	entrance
teaspoon	pellet	kindergarten
worrywart	klutz	restaurant
developer	envoy	functionary
shopaholic	postpone	dodge
magma	wafer	iota
briefcase	software	gelato
deputy	factoid	hankering
mangrove	marvelous	esteem
enfranchise	OR marvellous	knack
kiln	evince	satisfactory
webisode	season	barefoot
kangaroo	horizon	trope
Romeo	arborio	knock
emerge	cartoon	whittle

Cruising the Airwaves

The first broadcast of the Bee wasn't on television — it was on radio! It wasn't until 1946 that it was first televised. ESPN started airing the Scripps National Spelling Bee in 1994.

---

joyful	giggle	coercive
genuine	bowie	bailiff
recluse	teemed	infiltrate
shield	soppiness	skirmish
tiger	bask	constituent
romaine	lateral	flounder
migraine	usher	cleave
oasis	prone	millionaire
navigator	selfie	concrete
humane	skydiving	slurry
polenta	memes	heiress
delicacy	nuggets	reign
noggin	frailty	spectral
background	sweltering	dialect
thistle	scrounge	heist
***althorn	praise	avenue
Spaniel	scripture	pending
kilt	ulna	ewe
whirlybird	fellowship	stagestruck
Hungary	amass	standee
welding	missive	sailage
aforesaid	jitterbug	yoo-hoo
varnish	kennel	profiteer
spindle	heavenly	kernel
wheedle	shindig	tawny
whelp	melody	scalp
yonder	membership	scrapple
riffraff	oblong	nominee
restive	yammer	martial
various	whereas	acumen

***Beginning at this point, all the words remaining in the One Bee section are new to the 2021 version of *Words of the Champions*.

infirm
bleary
attitude
beseech
sunseeker
cornily
contraction
scooter
acceptance
rugby

shore
yippee
wand
Merlin
carnation
neaten
depose
frock
camcorder
gossip

version
fluid
vlogging
diversity
spangled
barbie
delta
handyman
stewardship
gruel

groom
trice
brick
privet
debunk
ballad
chide
atonement
citation
hardtack

rabid
teenagers
peat
harrowing
hobble
peddle
effortless
moped
groats
Highlands

Guinness World Record Holders

Did you know the 2019 Octochamps hold a Guinness World Record for Most winners of the Scripps National Spelling Bee in a single competition? Prior to 2019, the most winners there had ever been at a single event was two – most recently in 2016.

Difficulty Level: Two Bee
School Spelling Bee Study List

antsy	bridge	flurry
hover	pinpoint	glisten
billow	wisdom	accuse
posh	slate	drowsy
Canada	drape	scoff
toga	countless	opposite
bison	hideout	instrument
strum	ruins	blissfully
dangerous	Mexico	coarse
pluck	glazed	activists
squid	scanner	commute
Frisbee	oncoming	cocoa
teeter	flimsy	nutrients
chives	launch	scarcely
rallies	rubble	stretcher
pastry	tourists	lairs
coveralls	laughter	hybrid
ponytail	window	mustard
clatter	meeting	cruel
snout	plush	schedule
tumbling	helmet	goblins
cradle	whimper	splutter
firefly	bracelet	convince
serious	inwardly	grateful
banners	mobility	gesture
humor	eddy	formation
OR *humour	fanged	previous
mention	bough	imposing
spoken	listlessly	complicated
record	cautioned	unnoticed

*chiefly British spelling

agreement
dappled
rustle
chef
crease
whales
mislead
subtitles
fragment
retreat

implore
lento
Scandinavia
haggis
dolce
opus
pedestrian
snorkels
lullaby
FORTRAN

tangents
expression
violin
binary
semicolon
patent
incantations
treble
Baltic
ventured

deities
feta
proverb
indecipherable
podium
terraced
Aztec
laboratory
sinister
runes

ancestors
convulsive
jasper
berth
deference
detergent
sheathed
mantle
streamlet
strait

congratulate
fountain
curtly
garish
gilded
contingent
swerve
president
depths
Oregon
purpose

A Big Time Spellebrity
If you've watched the Bee on ESPN, you've probably seen his face. You've definitely heard his voice. We're talking about the official pronouncer of the Bee, Dr. Jacques Bailly. He won the Scripps National Spelling Bee in 1980 and took up the role of pronouncer in 2003.

Difficulty Level: Two Bee
Words of the Champions

hexagonal	choreographer	inundate
litmus	leguminous	wunderkind
seethe	ceramics	filial
antiquarian	mimetic	wearisome
phalanges	unabated	visage
bachelorette	petrifying	fascinator
frontier	specimen	testimony
unctuous	interlocutor	beaucoup
fluoride	machete	banal
moorage	dulcet	seismologist
Minotaur	salubrious	spectacles
intermezzo	rotisserie	innovator
edification	**paneer	bursary
vacuousness	OR panir	hallowed
epilepsy	omnibus	apogee
importunate	biscotti	hiatus
recuperation	calibrate	freesia
citronella	appellation	exoneration
palliative	duodenum	duvet
abhorrence	valorous	turpitude
personnel	isotopic	platitude
vexatious	carpal	nobiliary
faux	quizzical	commerce
sophisticated	heliotrope	keratitis
nebulous	squander	honorific
genus	prenuptial	kookaburra
legionnaire	succulent	napoleon
sternutation	bedraggled	superlative
subcutaneous	rectitude	oxygenate
alacrity	uranium	annihilate

**preferred spelling

sarcophagus
surrogate
terabyte
uncouth
onerous
macrocosm
bulbous
umpirage
heredity
philharmonic

endorphin
pharmacy
fondant
cupola
herbaceous
tentativeness
pachinko
decrepitude
redux
dramaturgy

murmuration
Clydesdale
phonics
calisthenics
obediential
odiferous
combination
torrent
arsenic
invertebrate

**bandanna
OR bandana
manipulable
axiomatic
indefatigable
ulterior
oligarchy
pianola
dignify
allegiance

basaltic
scorpion
planetarium
ecstatic
cinnamon
pharaoh
opponency
referendum
quaver
rabbinic

lapel
mackerel
callow
biscuit
flourish
beatific
repository
dissipate
accomplice
kerchief

whimsical
stamina
criteria
reprieve
consequent
contusion
mulligan
sabermetrics
elocution
dowager

comparison
diaphanous
agoraphobia
buffet
tortoise
surmountable
endure
bonobo
abrogate
effusive

primitive
fabulist
comportment
taciturn
sophomoric
laureate
Goliath
splenetic
legato
slovenly

Our Purpose
The purpose of the Bee is to help students improve their spelling, increase their vocabularies, learn concepts and develop correct English usage that will help them all their lives.

aerobics
paisley
contrariwise
petroleum
regalia
incinerate
flagon
incoherent
tercentenary
vituperative

churlish
riviera
laconic
excision
emblazoned
bric-a-brac
longitude
maverick
retrograde
partridge

insignia
binomial
luminance
adjective
elucidate
spatula
triglycerides
stalwart
bumptious
farcical

ghastly
parkour
fealty
perilous
steroid
gullibility
tarantula
cantankerous
vitriolic
crinoline

debris
armaments
versatile
subtlety
hangar
verbena
zirconium
ventriloquy
circumflex
calligram

eczema
theomachy
fibula
aberration
necrotic
eminent
demographics
Jurassic
myoglobin
frugal

achromatic
miscible
soprano
cutis
hyrax
truncheon
educand
Realtor
billabong
bariatrics

throughout
propulsion
assailant
charioteer
solicit
melismatic
spurious
tempeh
statistician
ibuprofen

injurious
anglophile
defiant
substitute
quiddity
karst
Brigadoon
vestibule
ballyhooed
arpeggio

lupine	alpaca	filbert
resuscitate	duress	Galahad
approbatory	eucalyptus	jadeite
catalepsy	rambunctious	peripheral
labyrinthine	ingenuous	elevator
notoriety	phonetician	chaperonage
subterranean	macular	frittata
aubergine	simpatico	vandalize
jalapeño	adhesion	chancellor
attributive	rennet	pauper
plutonomy	pinnacle	epoch
lobotomy	avalanche	dumbwaiter
assumption	cadge	allergenic
entrepreneur	exodus	vocabulary
besieged	philosophize	vassal
placoderm	Requiem	panary
hermitage	glitterati	tangerine
permutation	transference	pervasive
conference	uveal	haphazard
woebegone	candelabrum	legislature
resplendence	vacillate	shenanigans
aphasia	phenotype	inclusion
environs	transposable	physicists
celebratory	thrasonical	tempura
cornucopia	trepanation	reggae
prominent	Holstein	futility
archetype	quadrillion	untenable
travails	tardigrade	feudalism
antipathy	varsity	malevolent
leviathan	scholarship	posada

Sharing the Spotlight

The Scripps National Spelling Bee has declared co-champions in 1950, 1957, 1962, 2014, 2015, 2016 and 2019. Diana Reynard and Colquitt Dean were the first co-champs in 1950.

---

acquiesce
apothecary
summary
brogue
suet
koto
jingoism
satchel
evanescent
diverge

exemplar
marsupial
trefoil
designer
leisure
vague
wharf
altercation
fratority
cataclysmic

metatarsal
bereavement
carbohydrates
sesame
palatable
gratis
nonvolatile
juvenilia
fomentation
reprisal

astrobleme
sabotage
absolution
rutabaga
espousal
virulence
allocable
effraction
limousine
drupiferous

organelle
osprey
elusive
disproportionate
cayenne
tabernacle
phosphorescent
anxiety
conch
singultus

impromptu
oracle
condemn
scenographer
neuroticism
cannoli
platoon
solstice
swannery
probative

oblique
buoyancy
situation
lumbar
topiary
reverberant
yeanling
homicide
graphologist
principality

Nostradamus
taxonomic
beret
talisman
impecunious
reciprocity
molecule
millennial
ineffable
abnegation

beguile
centenary
matrimony
errata
stipulate
naïveté
OR naiveté
cadence
fido
vehicular

sabbatical	muchacha	affront
ermine	steppe	element
pugilist	palpitant	desolate
tapioca	nonchalance	truncate
festooned	realm	pedicure
tectonic	estuary	**caftan
wizened	technician	OR kaftan
tomfoolery	dietetic	ingratiate
harrumph	homage	sousaphone
embezzlement	cumulus	amalgam
fallacy	essential	carnage
asylum	seraphic	turmeric
remuneration	cameist	zoolatry
expostulate	scrumptiously	ricochet
integument	toploftical	hackneyed
Hebrides	noctambulist	vespertine
macaw	visibility	**brusque
perspicacious	ligament	OR brusk
reimbursable	plenitude	erstwhile
jambalaya	illustrious	lolled
geriatric	symmetrical	osteopath
striation	pendulous	kaiser
Appaloosa	analepsis	imperious
ramifications	mitigative	Egyptian
temerity	pyrite	foible
egress	sacrifice	lousicide
geocaching	consternation	ewer
instigate	escalator	curfew
obscure	impasto	schism
transcription	antagonistic	dilapidated

**preferred spelling

Who Knew?
The Scripps National Spelling Bee is the nation's largest and longest-running educational program.

peony
urgency
bifurcate
drivel
jettison
Promethean
embassy
contemptuous
okapi
welterweight

scrooge
morose
osmosis
flimflammer
astringent
mademoiselle
nouveau
heterochromia
consul
hermetically

excursion
dreadlocks
theriatrics
cumbersome
affluent
chastise
colic
atomic
fêng shui
acuity

subliminal
charismatic
phoenix
bastion
edamame
porcelain
deglaciation
recruit
tableau
sheldrake

suitable
cenotaph
Plumeria
perpetrator
cinematic
wallaby
contrivance
suffrage
thyme
phlebotomy

anemic
OR anaemic
depravity
effervescent
soirée
OR soiree
churros
diadem
larceny
acetaminophen

parochial
earnestly
**gaffe
OR gaff
ostensibly
shazam
gingivitis
patience
quittance
tenement

soothsayer
varicose
adage
cicada
mauve
emeritus
suture
obfuscate
casualty
perseverance

apparatus
myopic
ebullience
clairvoyance
impetus
affianced
archaism
commodious
austere
severance

**preferred spelling

financier	inimical	alma mater
wildebeest	kaleidoscope	comedienne
asado	gluttonous	cutaneous
limpa	gypsum	gnarled
adolescence	polypeptide	hydroponic
menagerie	wushu	combustible
hallucinate	contradictory	factorial
opprobrious	penitentiary	dolma
nocturnal	umbrage	sapphire
redolent	crustaceans	prevenient
vendage	bubonic	Edenic
entente	sartorial	tributary
boomslang	escarpment	laudatory
circuitous	Celsius	jitney
veracity	dialysis	wattage
marionette	humidistat	papillon
Neapolitan	sardonic	vertigo
chintzy	braille	accumulate
genteel	vignette	deltoidal
requisition	adjudicate	opulent
stimuli	caricature	paramecium
schooner	emerald	monochrome
declamatory	liege	facade
embryo	wilco	OR façade
languorous	germane	evaporation
stevia	bacteriolytic	bittern
phycology	rhododendron	flotsam
malaise	ineptitude	discombobulate
staid	academese	scrutiny
acerbity	registrar	concatenate

Did You Know?

In 2002, the Bee introduced the written test at the national finals for the first time. The vocabulary portion of the test came along in 2013.

impeachable
residue
halibut
spectrometer
circadian
servitude
traverse
tungsten
vineyard
interrogative

proletarian
vantage
discountenance
stupefy
irrevocable
trellis
juxtapose
hydrangea
slalom
corollary

adieu
tenaciously
indemnity
cyanosis
regurgitate
stegosaur
statuesque
nectarine
galvanize
agonistic

scullery
tiramisu
exaggerate
enoki
profundity
mantra
escarole
nanotechnology
bureau
burglarious

étude
cranium
equivalent
portentous
nepotism
truffle
varicella
tonsillitis
thoracic
proviso

rosin
burial
bulwark
iridescent
quince
cyclone
usurper
phraseology
caramel
pecuniary

cryptozoa
preponderance
bruxism
psychoanalysis
calendar
reiterate
remorseful
cybernetics
garniture
twilight

netiquette
paucity
doldrums
slumgullion
valedictorian
auspices
elaborative
proprietary
**nascent
OR naissant

cornea
resilience
apiary
ronin
tropical
pontiff
omniscient
capacity
sewage
epoxy

**preferred spelling

discreetly	berserk	tandoori
sieve	cathedral	succumb
trounce	deciduous	fervently
hydrophobia	baleen	divestiture
ingot	Einstein	roseola
nubuck	municipal	installation
jocularity	adversaria	harbinger
unfurl	turbinado	raptatorial
calculator	brethren	sobriety
corduroy	tympanum	manumit
encore	fisticuffs	dentifrice
hollyhock	propinquity	collegiality
qualms	epidermis	inclement
mosaic	carriage	celery
centipede	abstemious	idiosyncratic
attendee	echinoderm	burgoo
nomenclature	optimum	occupancy
botany	pathogen	coriander
Holocaust	acrostic	amnesty
augment	anthropology	condensation
acoustic	cruciferous	aqueduct
eruption	macchiato	ferret
auburn	ancillary	widdershins
virtually	toile	hostile
glissando	plaudits	subsequent
stomach	serenade	whet
demonstrative	heptad	blatant
megalomaniac	engineer	pyramid
posse	pilcrow	terminus
declension	porosity	agitation

tremulous
scythe
duplicitous
protectorate
placards
corral
credulity
dissonance
shoji
auditorium

reconcilable
evaluate
mastodon
denticulate
supplicate
torsion
justiciable
vernal
aardvark
census

stagflation
brontophobia
macrobiotics
glareous
rejuvenate
tubular
dodecahedron
rictus
vengeance
modular

kleptocrat
neuropathy
surrealist
secession
digression
intricate
annotate
vehemence
fervorous
septennial

hypotenuse
emancipatory
supine
fracas
disrepair
photogenic
rehearsal
irritability
vainglorious
ataxia

pageantry
vinegar
fiduciary
emulsify
lorikeet
malfeasance
sequential
intersperse
numerology
Paleozoic

funnel
syndicate
chrysalis
bethesda
cartilage
coeval
curio
ombudsman
hydrant
zeppelin

superficiality
marooned
**volary
OR volery
follicle
brochure
grotesqueness
privatim
eradicate
krypton

ethanol
quadriceps
tachycardia
triceratops
sandal
pashmina
utilitarian
millivolt
herringbone
orchestra

**preferred spelling

phlox	boondoggle	wordmonger
tractability	phylum	wobbulator
montage	hypochondria	mahogany
compendium	obstetrician	moribund
unmoored	replete	recriminatory
yardang	raucous	subaqueous
fluctuation	Brandywine	recusancy
flabbergast	surreptitious	retrocedence
accolade	surplus	cauterize
connivery	impediment	immolate
impresario	revenant	résumé
bruschetta	topgallant	extensive
dictum	clandestine	transcend
premonition	genealogical	freneticism
stereotypical	pomposity	merino
bergamot	neonatology	pestilence
telepathic	pituitary	mordant
banquet	fleetness	posthumous
upbraid	anonymity	QWERTY
pancreas	carcinogenic	foosball
expunge	detritus	accentuate
maize	anorak	ascension
metastasize	enviable	venue
quintessential	extrapolate	microfiche
pollutant	extinguish	quadrilateral
brouhaha	pilaster	turpentine
pedantry	perceptible	cellophane
performance	dystopia	indulgent
equivocate	muesli	occipital
fission	crux	predicament

From Around the World

Most spellers at the Scripps National Spelling Bee are from the United States, but spellers also come from American Samoa, Guam, Puerto Rico, the U.S. Virgin Islands, Department of Defense Schools in Europe as well as the Bahamas, Canada, Ghana, Jamaica, Japan and South Korea.

provincial
antithesis
gouge
salivate
laity
indolent
documentary
bromide
algae
reminiscent

menial
Moroccan
clearance
assure
compatriots
liaise
quotidian
matriculation
revulsive
gaucho

capsule
tragedian
fajitas
felonious
palatial
Mecca
albeit
vermicide
echelon
supremacy

clowder
occultation
Chihuahua
promontory
shar-pei
narcoleptic
efface
sycophant
bellwether
clarinet

capillary
disposition
remonstrance
smithereens
curator
judicious
vice versa
exercise
civet
pancetta

waiver
decennial
dynamite
Gemini
retinol
corpulent
potpourri
pallor
Yorkshire
Belgravia

casserole
semester
sacrament
terra-cotta
moratorium
cognizant
OR *cognisant
languish
protuberant
chortle

unscathed
raclette
superstitious
mawkish
flambé
patronymic
odometer
uvula
enumerated
desertification

quirky
arraign
elegant
minacious
vindictive
implacable
logarithmic
regicide
hubris
hibernaculum

*chiefly British spelling

The First Bee
In 1925, the first national spelling bee was organized by the *Louisville Courier-Journal* with a total of nine spellers. Frank Neuhauser won the championship title after correctly spelling "gladiolus."

bandicoot
malinger
parliamentary
rebarbative
olympiad
crocodile
venerable
chemise
campanology
persuasible

desultorily
papyrus
El Niño
anchorage
conundrum
debilitate
mittimus
mellifluous
clemency
backgammon

intuitable
divvy
fatuously
fraudulent
necessity
piety
veritable
sashay
sciatica
discomfiture

emphysema
stridency
acetone
cerebellum
pantomime
prima donna
praxis
Tinseltown
sorrel
McCoy

histrionics
cashier
polysemy
stampede
forfeit
armadillo
overweening
sacrosanct
syringe
eclipse

espadrille
corgi
caffeine
panacea
cabaret
froufrou
eschew
ventricle
inducement
vanguard

portrait
tepidity
meridian
spontaneity
platinum
nonnegotiable
disparate
artifice
cymbals
nucleated

exorbitant
reparations
constabulary
speculate
stratosphere
noxious
arbitrary
quasar
Podunk
seize

pathos
equinox
prosperous
sclerosis
ablaut
anabolic
jimberjawed
toilsome
tempestuous
univocal

avarice
bouclé
OR boucle
thoroughbred
potassium
peculate
treatise
undergird
oompah
adulation

minutia
anticipatory
chinook
indigent
merganser
sternum
par excellence
thwartwise
tae kwon do
fenestrated

lugubrious
isosceles
hoity-toity
Mesopotamian
Muzak
vicinity
merely
abominable
procedure
limpid

syllabus
animus
trillium
Dalmatian
ufology
cholera
**minuscule
OR miniscule
jeepney
volucrine

populace
vetiver
parameters
inflammable
pyrotechnics
mollify
cohesive
stigmata
prolix
mitochondria

onomatopoeia
lavender
tensile
gaudery
luxuriate
cavalcade
gladiatorial
machination
pugnacious
peruse

alluvial
epicurean
derelict
revelation
arithmetic
depredation
ignominious
auction
assiduous
diligence

bodega
bona fide
gustatory
obliterate
legalese
rudiments
monitory
equilibrium
roustabout
trifle

ambrosial
simultaneity
gastronome
epithet
encroach
acacia
tetanus
scarlatina
ciao
genome

**preferred spelling

Did You Know?

The Scripps National Spelling Bee was featured in the Academy Award-nominated documentary *Spellbound*.

inviolable
contrite
patrician
enervate
turophile
Patagonia
vanquish
ectoplasm
olfactory
en masse

stroganoff
procrastinate
purification
plantain
aperture
rhythmically
ludicrous
bountiful
pantheon
marimba

conduit
bravado
beneficent
indict
epitome
annulment
vegetarian
surimi
besmirch
trespass

commandeer
bonsai
university
celestial
preposterous
extant
cogently
auricular
settee
legitimately

inoculate
heleoplankton
pliant
billiards
obstreperous
frabjous
spiracle
Formica
Mylar
rustication

globular
stellular
akimbo
derisive
ineluctable
eerily
funambulist
apotheosis
entrée
homeostasis

calamari
prehensile
somatotype
bizarro
dissemble
gallant
intensify
hurriedly
corrosive
afghan

odontiasis
stratification
tomahawk
artesian
mendacious
gubernatorial
pungent
mandrill
gibbous
extracurricular

punctuation
nautilus
thievery
dragoon
yuzu
ritziness
gazette
continuum
pachyderm
symposium

floribunda
salience
molasses
classical
fungible
Gothamite
affable
dopamine
pitiful
ammunition

pariah
prodigious
denominator
prorogue
fecund
laceration
nexus
decor
OR décor
duchy

pagoda
establishment
ruminate
sympathy
puniness
lingua franca
triforium
**déjà vu
OR déjà vue
calabash

**chute
OR shute
impermeable
trepidation
collision
scarab
veganism
humerus
vagabonds
variegated

volition
gossamer
vincible
factitious
sculpture
annuity
quid pro quo
curmudgeon
cushion
tutelage

domiciled
theorem
accrual
grandeur
ottoman
logographic
armistice
cryogenic
catalyst
thespian

submersible
extemporaneous
ungetatable
unilaterally
ordinance
ursine
arduous
carnitas
bulgogi
fibromyalgia

terrier
captivated
onus
precursor
mochi
feign
dementia
voilà
OR voila
habanero

Francophone
convivium
atrium
italicization
preliminary
echoed
reticulated
authenticate
fiscal
oblige

**preferred spelling

viscount
plague
preferential
bazooka
complacency
kraken
stanzaic
putrescent
nostalgia
dechlorinate

unconscionable
Pembroke
liquefaction
palazzo
miasma
concoct
modicum
javelin
spoonerism
complicit

gyrocopter
**medieval
OR mediaeval
licensure
Herculean
pilgrimages
oriel
preeminent
alfresco
loquacious

prosthetic
latency
epitaphs
solitaire
dishevel
Limburger
tuffet
epact
abstruse
nephrolith

adipose
quorum
pharynx
epistolary
pursuit
esoteric
grapheme
trigonometry
alloy
Belgium

audacious
exasperate
Mandarin
Kelvin
vellum
enunciate
tarsier
autodidact
parable
rowan

tripartite
Bohemian
succinct
inquietude
compunction
decumbiture
multivalent
artillery
quotient
ricotta

guttural
atrocious
vivacious
xenoglossy
smorgasbord
electrode
sporadically
sudation
cytoplasm
affectionately

Pulitzer
vitreous
wraith
insulin
phlegmatic
spasmodic
bouquet
denizen
duopoly
alpinist

**preferred spelling

abracadabra	abhenry	jonquil
plethora	chromosome	pensive
rappelled	braggart	quarantine
conceit	relentlessly	schnitzel
tapas	opalescence	rialto
sediment	polyglot	delphinium
emulate	velociraptor	obelisk
caveat	puree	diurnal
doubloons	manticore	prejudice
oscillation	chronometer	bombastic
enzyme	cherubic	cistern
dinero	wherewithal	exquisite
comestibles	inquisitor	epsilon
stenographer	chemistry	petroglyphs
mezzanine	quandary	specious
lozenge	equanimity	pumice
tedious	thermos	zodiac
resonate	acrylics	artery
suspicion	imminent	ornithology
repudiate	hieroglyphics	apropos
emporium	oculus	pessimum
Victorian	dubiously	amateurish
forestallment	mariposa	**intransigent
Iberian	teleology	OR intransigeant
fluency	bowyer	tyrannical
invective	infatuation	pearlescent
occur	abysmal	tautology
claustrophobia	chambray	misconstrue
idyllic	rhombus	sagacious
coralline	revendicate	mammalian

**preferred spelling

There's a First Time for Everything

Hugh Tosteson was the first winner from outside of the fifty U.S. states.
He lived in Puerto Rico.

---

tranquil
behemoth
equestrian
nominal
draconian
trebuchet
ransom
iambic
monocle
apocalypse

cemetery
anticoagulant
euro
Gouda
endocrine
presumptuous
doubt
unkempt
cursive
binoculars

apportion
gurney
sanctimonious
peremptory
infarction
cedar
udon
gourd
verbatim
joule

niacin
courage
arabesque
cylindrical
tephra
lackadaisical
silhouette
dismal
consortium
tuition

multifarious
unanimous
soporific
tupelo
cadaverous
prowess
dromedary
squalid
tracheotomy
firmament

paramountcy
sultana
agrarian
collapsar
exhibition
ministrations
racketeer
solder
interim
definiendum

***dandle
effete
Antigua
vaudeville
frisket
brockage
malapropism
pelf
aqueous
Dianthus

olingo
Halifax
concordance
huerta
vascular
wentletrap
serrated
poblano
conclave
Gregorian

rebuff
taverna
illicitly
cribbage
crith
Namibian
tricenary
triste
interred
legerity

***Beginning at this point, all the words
remaining in the Two Bee section are new to the
2021 version of *Words of the Champions*.

Vatican	grandiloquent	château
fucoid	armature	erroneous
parley	maidenhair	tam-o'-shanter
meningitis	aureole	trillado
nutation	spinosity	per se
nutria	prespinous	peradventure
sedge	cladistics	Ryeland
capstan	gasiform	domesticity
vicarious	valuator	episcopal
alate	deserter	consecrate
victimology	jankers	trituration
ibex	Evactor	neoterism
cudgel	possessive	interregnum
bicameral	venial	viaticum
irrigation	seton	homiletics
labradoodle	demerits	psalmody
portico	diaspora	omnilegent
corsage	pious	princeps
smellfungus	borough	procurement
arboretum	volatile	cribo
Zamboni	gnocchi	colubrine
blarney	surety	immie
diacritic	pileus	aretalogy
mephitic	fez	sessile
complementary	glengarry	du jour
Philistine	commissioner	lanceolate
dyspeptic	grande dame	bowsprit
inglorious	verism	Charon
louche	dramatization	chupacabra
avatar	nonconformist	Acadians

Gippsland
froward
ensconced
cattalo
OR catalo
hypogeous

Eight Times the Fun
In 2019, eight spellers made Bee history and inspired a neologism: "Octochamps!" At about midnight on the night of the Finals, the dictionary admitted defeat to what the Bee declared "the most phenomenal assemblage of spellers in the history of this storied competition." Rishik Gandhasri, Erin Howard, Saketh Sundar, Shruthika Padhy, Sohum Sukhatankar, Abhijay Kodali, Christopher Serrao and Rohan Raja ended the 2019 Bee in an eight-way tie.

Difficulty Level: Three Bee
School Spelling Bee Study List

cladding
scallion
stealthily
warden
copious
hurtle
fester
intoxicating
outlandish
porcupine

lurching
ineffective
trough
parchment
leach
wrath
corporate
propane
dissuade
profusion

appalling
divulge
meditation
franchise
pretentious
embellishes
appropriate
rummages
constricting
inevitable

engrossed
strife
hindmost
eviction
protruding
substantial
hooey
blight
fronds
authority

minimize
OR *minimise
**flamingos
OR flamingoes
mechanics
bankrupt
insurance
dismayed
offspring
pillage

anguish
increments
Odin
parishioner
astrologers
devout
shrike
Vancouver
conjure
stalagmite

traitorous
condominium
impenetrable
intercede
defector
livery
scuttlebutt
battalion
chalet
Lutheran

roiling
psychiatrist
disconcerting
Jesuit
fodder
sinuously
irreversible
barricade
moustache
OR mustache

unprepossessing
bipolar
torpid
featherbrained
immoderate
arrayed
countenance
scepter
OR *sceptre
scourge

*chiefly British spelling
**preferred spelling

irreverent
apparition
dosages
superintendent
exhalation
discord
clamorous
grimaces
inheritance
plumage

epaulet
OR epaulette
propound
chauffeurs
disconsolate
testosterone
minivets
proscenium
politesse
chanteuse

arrondissement
carabinieri
tamarisk
liana
sibilant
au revoir
bitumen
sacristy
Salzkammergut
frisson

Aachen
oriole
Ganges
niagara
carrion
samosas
chalice
necromancer
proffered
colonel

subaltern
Etruscan
cloisters
redound
Benedictine
arcane
soleil
copse
scabbard
courtiers

assuage
adjutant
inexorably
disgorged
Algiers
primavera
souterrain
knickerbockers
litany
unsullied

Carthusian
**maharaja
OR maharajah
**Upanishads
OR Upanisads
arret
marquee

**preferred spelling

Bee's Bookshelf

The Bee's Bookshelf is the official online book club of the Scripps National
Spelling Bee. It's a place to explore the connection between stories and spelling.
Each month, we read a new book together and share insights, so sign up to
receive our monthly emails to find out which book is next. Visit
spellingbee.com/bookshelf to learn more.

Difficulty Level: Three Bee
Words of the Champions

imaret	sumpsimus	umami
cornichon	morel	persiflage
devastavit	abeyance	toreador
Mediterranean	rongeur	vermicelli
longevous	mountebank	frangipane
digerati	allelopathy	reseau
solecism	capoeira	moulage
hypertrophy	agnolotti	interpellate
ravigote	ballabile	genuflect
inchoate	draegerman	cinerarium
judoka	prescient	polemic
vaccary	Fribourg	paladin
Adelaide	proselytizer	totipotency
unwonted	OR *proselytiser	agnomen
tazza	tenon	Bauhaus
damson	nubilous	sacerdotal
pelisse	iatrogenic	skeuomorph
succade	onychitis	binturong
tumulus	roux	mamushi
dorsiflexor	tuatara	lipophilic
profiterole	chicle	codicil
valetudinary	sulcus	coulomb
aristoi	thalamus	violaceous
vireo	gyttja	Rorschach
rococo	jibboom	arthralgia
lachsschinken	vestigial	desman
wakame	Orwellian	jacaranda
bathos	gimbaled	huapango
nihilism	cabaletta	predilection
ustion	hesped	entomophagy

*chiefly British spelling

paronomasia
facsimile
renminbi
interferon
sedulous
velouté
Aesopian
frigate
enoptromancy
satiety

perorate
danseur
chevalier
taurine
hierurgical
melee
emolument
ikebana
exaugural
gaillardia

caryatid
heliacal
schefflera
contrapposto
temblor
insouciance
catarrh
quattrocento
millegrain
canaille

verisimilitude
Keynesian
akaryote
azulejo
hauberk
bouillon
tarpaulin
cephalopod
pulchritude
pekoe

patois
Rubicon
bourgeois
aerophilatelic
ankh
contumelious
vicissitudes
lilliputian
Sbrinz
kathakali

cozen
oxalis
myeloma
lebensraum
mufti
dirigible
surcease
ascetic
oolite
revanche

megrims
podagra
palaver
luthier
yttriferous
vermeil
Ouagadougou
bibliopegist
plagiarism
holobenthic

boutonniere
anodyne
saccharide
boulevardier
quokka
lidocaine
contretemps
a posteriori
scaberulous
anaglyphy

reconnoiter
OR reconnoitre
realpolitik
colloque
onychorrhexis
paraffin
vigneron
tannined
spiedini
anhinga

jai alai
Rastafarian
succussion
avifauna
joropo
toxicosis
colporteur
OR colporter
agitprop
Achernar

cassock
meringue
mackinaw
sambal
yuloh
hermeneutics
tikkun
macaque
lassitude
oeuvre

altazimuth
Castilian
trichinosis
ecclesiology
teppanyaki
cicatrize
somnolent
intonaco
realia
grison

phulkari
garrulous
paroxysm
communiqué
Chantilly
jacquard
sorghum
guilloche
appositive
dirndl

latke
martinet
asterion
hypallage
solenoid
veridical
threnody
Jacobean
ballotage
ocotillo

dubitante
disciform
mizuna
trichotillomania
huipil
mustelid
prestidigitation
soupçon
diphtheria
bdelloid

nugatory
commorients
immiscible
toroidal
bialy
appurtenances
corsair
zabaglione
velamen
sporran

clematis
kente
ranine
riparian
**accoutrement
OR accouterment
radicchio
dudgeon
nitid
Basenji

concinnate
Stradivarius
synecdoche
tulsi
sebaceous
papeterie
litigious
phytophilous
meunière
hilum

**preferred spelling

One Dictionary to Rule them All
The only source for the Scripps National Spelling Bee is the Merriam-Webster Unabridged Online Dictionary. (http://unabridged.merriam-webster.com/)

fanfaronade
malachite
urticaria
capsaicin
ptosis
pejerrey
horologist
speleothem
euripus
samarium

variscite
bolide
vervain
chanoyu
hamadryad
calumny
escabeche
ad hominem
oubliette
béchamel

repoussage
otacoustic
naranjilla
elegiac
pâtissier
OR patissier
Yeatsian
surfeit
limicolous
girandole

googol
étagère
anechoic
leonine
laulau
Gruyère
proprioceptive
oppugn
macropterous
euphonious

retinoscopy
sepulchral
sangfroid
pasilla
maringouin
argot
vicenary
ajimez
pompeii
oviparous

mangonel
coalescence
Plantagenet
bauxite
kakapo
pelagial
ague
largesses
fulgent
olecranon

toreutics
mascarpone
rissole
seneschal
pinniped
wahine
grissino
coterie
sylph
katsura

diastole
mediobrome
demurrage
tristeza
trigeminal
bruja
upsilon
sakura
buccal
zocalo

**aficionado
OR afficionado
piscivorous
benison
gagaku
amygdala
scurrilous
flèche
tetrachoric
sforzando

thalassic
frazil
rapprochement
glacis
ahimsa
kanji
weltschmerz
jalousie
ichthyology
pruritus

dactylic
affogato
scrivener
dysrhythmia
dragée
choucroute
hsaing-waing
stevedore
harangue
niveau

rouille
rescissible
Jungian
Groenendael
facile
chrysolite
execrable
hangul
cartouches
Nicoise
OR Niçoise

julienne
moiety
pastitsio
modiste
deuterium
Icarian
pappardelle
Sahel
bibelot
telegnosis

loupe
oleiculture
**loess
OR löss
ruelle
Ushuaia
redingote
adscititious
hummock
internecine

duxelles
mesial
Feldenkrais
bailiwick
bozzetto
coiffure
repartee
chimera
OR *chimaera
avgolemono

exiguous
presentient
renvoi
kichel
semaphore
gambol
angiitis
Teutonic
Conestoga
zeitgeist

heinousness
nacelle
rupicolous
Pythagorean
kepi
**bulgur
OR bulghur
ushabti
puchero
nival

ascites
Véronique
OR Veronique
planetesimal
taoiseach
obeisant
whippoorwill
Ficus
agelicism
subrident

*chiefly British spelling
**preferred spelling

It's All Greek to Me

We often get questions about why we use words that may not appear to be English. Most words in the English language are words that we borrowed from other languages. We borrowed them, used them, and now call them our own.

ethylene
flaneur
Ponzi
teneramente
styptic
sopapilla
nictitate
boutade
towhee
escritoire

affenpinscher
gudgeon
beaumontage
galoot
desiccate
aporia
moraine
hirsute
shubunkin
hepatectomy

bloviate
seine
galapago
au courant
crepuscular
theca
croustade
kipuka
noumenon
chicanery

vilipend
vitiate
spodumene
leberwurst
daguerreotype
yakitori
pejorate
Aitutakian
parterre
rondeau

atlatl
allochroous
ennui
caisson
cheongsam
graticule
gyascutus
cygnet
supercilious
dysphasia

kugel
topazolite
trompe l'oeil
ailette
fetticus
rocaille
couverture
lemniscus
ad nauseam
ganache

sauger
kanban
toccata
pertinacity
gasthaus
transmontane
laterigrade
hyssop
naumachia
focaccia

pahoehoe
Kjeldahl
rubefacient
halcyon
corrigenda
Zanni
nonage
beurre
jicama
sturnine

octonocular
parallax
antenatus
trouvaille
glazier
kinesiology
exogenous
aniseikonia
guayabera
realgar

anaphylaxis
bobolink
diluent
urushiol
andouille
otiose
megacephalic
souchong
poltroon
Freudian

floruit
Bunyanesque
exsect
champignon
bahuvrihi
panjandrum
catachresis
tiffin
colcannon
tournedos

ormolu
blottesque
consommé
OR consomme
ullage
zortzico
teratism
flagellum
panegyric
hoi polloi

sirenian
nescience
blatherskite
consigliere
adiabatic
camembert
ecchymosis
oppidan
decastich
Naugahyde

lefse
beccafico
amphistylar
saturnine
zaibatsu
titian
tokonoma
unguiculate
amaryllis
reveille

regnal
attaché
rafflesia
ranunculus
pistou
scintillation
Bolognese
farrago
coup de grace
tourelle

notturno
ginglymus
hemorrhage
tapetum
golem
krewe
toque
avuncular
habiliments
rubato

gentilitial
obnebulate
allonym
croquembouche
kobold
mendicity
castellated
toponymic
boudin
bucatini

reboation
haupia
Keplerian
codswallop
hauteur
camarilla
nidicolous
oxyacetylene
queue
hellebore

transhumance	coaxation	luculent
phloem	ardoise	expatiate
lacustrine	farouche	xerogel
ageusia	farfalle	vizierial
pillor	ogival	crescive
deleterious	stretto	tryptophan
ikat	coccygeal	neophyte
pylorus	Diplodocus	buffa
erythroblast	tachyon	clavichord
maillot	piccata	de rigueur
epenthesis	isagoge	secant
hinoki	élan	comanchero
nonpareil	breviloquence	meiosis
nyctinasty	kalimba	gules
pointelle	illative	nimiety
vinaigrette	betony	lokelani
tinnient	bêtise	psoriasis
aioli	transience	bavardage
pochoir	frison	coulibiac
glyceraldehyde	flavedo	xyloglyphy
hagiographer	maquillage	Aramaic
syncope	mortadella	anathema
icosahedron	stanchion	basilica
goanna	spirulina	rajpramukh
wassail	eleemosynary	Chalcolithic
ammonite	force majeure	rinceau
tanager	ossicle	filar
pneumatocyst	anemone	bhangra
fortissimo	alpargata	risorgimento
portmanteau	disembogue	agalma

Home Sweet Home
While many people think the Bee is headquartered in Washington, D.C., our hive is actually located in Cincinnati, Ohio.

analgesia
dengue
cantatrice
emollient
parquet
dhurrie
lapidary
cachexia
connoisseur
ferruginous

gendarme
demulcent
goosander
kwashiorkor
lecithin
cetology
plenipotentiary
foudroyant
sesquipedalian
expugnable

profligacy
yosenabe
funori
piloncillo
xiphias
étouffée
OR etouffee
degauss
tussock
lanolated

linnet
embouchure
plangency
apocryphal
tamarack
puerilely
obloquy
dhole
**budgerigar
OR budgereegah
OR budgerygah

outré
ululate
sororal
epideictic
embolus
caveola
farina
heuristic
nudibranch
triquetra

paramahamsa
duello
fjeld
tomography
effleurage
chastushka
bergère
Erewhonian
rhyton
orogeny

Pepysian
esplanade
gesellschaft
tamari
arenaceous
panettone
tmesis
clerihew
tsukupin
katakana

Parmentier
rugose
brume
hiortdahlite
extravasate
incunabula
cordillera
zazen
cabochon
après

zydeco
consanguine
bibimbap
aquiclude
demitasse
tomalley
bouffant
bas-relief
rhizome
Wensleydale

erubescent	peregrination	auteur
estovers	paraquat	labefaction
rembrandt	prana	ibidem
bonspiel	sinciput	estival
hackamore	abattoir	OR aestival
blancmange	glossopetrae	loup-garou
simulacrum	diktat	empennage
cnidarian	llanero	lysozyme
capotasto	Machiavellian	grimthorpe
Panagia	glaucomatous	thaumaturge
nockerl	haori	pinioned
rhabdoid	rheostat	fouetté
apodyterium	hariolation	venenate
apoplexy	thylacine	badinage
verdure	cenote	saccadic
fait accompli	griffonage	mignonette
dreikanter	fossiliferous	coadjutor
penicillin	calefacient	chiffonade
pendeloque	obdurate	haricot
beelzebub	nunchaku	Luddite
rhinorrhagia	senryu	wickiup
foley	cormorant	nisse
syzygy	gnomon	impugn
Beethovenian	pinetum	brouillon
tatterdemalion	brucellosis	derecho
susurrus	wasteweir	solipsist
**bienvenue	diamanté	sinophile
OR bienvenu	sphygmometer	harmattan
potwalloper	**kibitzer	**incarnadine
kaffeeklatsch	OR kibbitzer	OR encarnadine

**preferred spelling

On a Global Scale

At just 12 years old, Jody-Anne Maxwell, from Kingston, Jamaica, was our first international champion. She won the Bee in 1998.

dulcinea
nainsook
querida
paillard
gazoz
Glaswegian
stannum
putsch
tralatitious
denouement

hortatory
maquette
obliviscence
autophagy
Airedale
potager
malleolus
*** marcel
croquignole
dolmen

griot
vexillologist
**halala
OR halalah
corybantic
chasuble
furuncle
pongee
acoel
acral

Koine
weka
haplography
Tchefuncte
becquerel
darnel
giallolino
krausen
Castalia
nahcolite

telamon
uraeus
teledu
gattine
mele
Marathi
nuciform
grandrelle
bordereaux
rambla

tullibee
guichet
Guarnerius
unakite
azotea
gabbro
gegenschein
hebdomadal
gypsophila
koh-i-noor

nocive
cataphora
blastema
trochee
diapason
deliquesce
aperçu
cioppino
inglenook
efflux

frugivore
lobscouse
senecio
jasmone
hawok
fructiferous
martinoe
lierre
porwigle
portugais

ligas
Osloite
sciolistic
seraya
janthina
Skeltonic
balata
balbriggan
affeer
pomology

**preferred spelling
***Beginning at this point, all the words
remaining in the Three Bee section are new to
the 2021 version of *Words of the Champions*.

coadjutor
Svengali
escheator
dogana
toorie
exchequer
habeas corpus
kerril
pudibund
toril
ryas

terai
gabarit
guerite
gallivat
charcuterie
zugzwang
triskelion
crokinole
anicca
batamote

yabbies
salmagundi
OR salmagundy
**hutia
OR jutia
Deseret
Djibouti
Tegucigalpa
Llullaillaco
Pyxis

**preferred spelling

Word Club

Want a new way to study? The Word Club app, available in the App Store and the Google Play Store, makes mastering *Words of the Champions* fun! Choose from multiple different quiz and study options for both spelling and vocabulary, all with expert audio pronunciations from the Bee's official pronouncer, Dr. Jacques Bailly.

About Scripps

The E.W. Scripps Company (NASDAQ: SSP) advances understanding of the world through journalism. As the nation's fourth-largest independent TV station owner, Scripps operates 60 television stations in 42 markets. Scripps empowers the next generation of news consumers with its multiplatform news network Newsy and reaches growing audiences through broadcast networks including Bounce and Court TV. Shaping the future of storytelling through digital audio, Scripps owns top podcast company Stitcher and Triton, the global leader in technology and measurement services. Scripps runs an award-winning investigative reporting newsroom in Washington, D.C., and is the longtime steward of the Scripps National Spelling Bee. Founded in 1878, Scripps has held for decades to the motto, "Give light and the people will find their own way."

2021 Words of the Champions
Copyright 2020, Scripps National Spelling Bee

Made in the USA
Las Vegas, NV
14 July 2021